AN ESCHATOLOGICAL BESTIARY

BY

OZ HARDWICK

Published by
Dog Horn Publishing
45 Monk Ings, Birstall, Batley WF17 9HU
United Kingdom
doghornpublishing.com

ISBN 978-1-907133-69-5

Artwork by
Oz Hardwick

Typesetting by
Jonathan Penton

UK Distribution: Central Books
99 Wallis Road, London, E9 5LN, United Kingdom
orders@centralbooks.com
Phone:+44 (0) 845 458 9911
Fax: +44 (0) 845 458 9912

Overseas Distribution: Printondemand-worldwide.com
9 Culley Court
Orton Southgate
Peterborough
PE2 6XD
Telephone: 01733 237867
Facsimile: 01733 234309
Email: info@printondemand-worldwide.com

First Edition published by Dog Horn Publishing, 2013

An Eschatological Bestiary

An Eschatological Bestiary admits to different foci. Recording descriptions of natural history and popular accounts of climate change and inequality, its faunal composition offers symbolic visions, modern protest, and a complete exegetical interpretation of the dramatic rise of an apparently semi-permanent moral blank. Among its prime concerns and other sediments of stories are power relations and future events, their primary goal being to render the Big System unstable at a local level. To this end, words cut out of other sources serve to embody allegorical versions of imaginary animals in literature and art, providing chance significance to each animal's common misconceptions. In addition to glacial analyses, therefore, this 'sea text dream collection' preserves a record (including tents) of data relating to prophetic processes in any town's financial district, revealing the value of bad practice.

Ape rejoices in windows which encourage personal devotion, from a Greek word meaning: "with funeral functions in hand." We may note that Ape loves and cares for others' pushed-in noses, thereby acting similarly to humans. Yet humorous anthropomorphism suffocates, while the Church's glance loves purely physical aspects of human life made pleasant. Two scrupulously self-examining Ape children represent the opposite: one is present when they sometimes accidentally kill during the new moon, the other says that they are only sad when in church. This is, no doubt, similar to the intellectual and moral inferiority of Ape when compared with men. Ape is delighted with so tight and fertile an embrace but, nevertheless, should be seen as spiritual wax, whilst at the same time stressing the need for diligent humility in the world outside. Hugging Ape acts as a reminder of the waning of the moon, but the neglected child survives because of the ugly hunters bound to earth. In Ape's aspirational phase, the concentration of the boot is nearest to the moon, unlike the others in almost all of its shaggy features. As Ape, lacking snares, still mimics the divine, so must man set out nooses and play at draughts.

Kingfisher is incapable of moving on work days. Stirred by little but chance, it troubles navigable time, nourishing numerous deceptive legends. When Kingfisher is enchanted by over-protective mothers charged with keeping the river near his eggs, he makes the women his nest, receives an incommunicable vision, and is joined by the daughters of all deceivers. Together, they will not assist the 'halcyon days' of Christ, particularly at table. Kingfisher proves himself by reducing speech to countless continuations; unfinished nature is, for him, a story of the calm appropriation of winter and the subsequent drawing of a new time. In mirroring widely, Kingfisher remains unnaturally calm, except around a resurgent midsummer hero. The most recent thinking in Kingfisher fertility treads this fine line, only to be occupied by the sea in which it sheds its feathers: on the strongest legs of storms, this becomes a barren wasteland. Kingfisher builds nests seven days before the sea grows calm, as well as inspiring scholarship concerning the shortest day. During the following fourteen days, the chosen martyrs who they breed are but fish in a can. A ritual seabird that is named after noble blood in mid-winter innocence, Kingfisher's song heralds wild, unruly measures.

Tiger is the tricky homewrecker. When judged by strong and swift mirrors, Tiger rages impotently, leaving mothers deforested but ready to mate. In straitened times, Tiger thinks every story you understand will be endangered, making children out of space in evolutionary terms. Yet Tiger remains the hunter of the nation, remarkably dangerous because of his glass spheres resembling language. Tiger's call is not created horrible, although scientists believe that, since the mainland flooded, its wild tail became so different that one long word with stripes may bridge the ancient gap between stupid and whore. Tiger confesses to mistakes, but in flight (like an arrow) has neither good qualities nor days. The swiftest is the colder species, although any association with a different environment is unlikely: surprising, shadow hunters are by no means home. For although fierce want lays claims wherever the hunter prepares to take life, the last Tiger may have given the climate to robbers. Tiger dismisses rumours and is admired for speed, only stopping to cancel the future. At a later date, Tiger may return to his territory, never more taking part in distinguished escapes, yet there will always remain a bizarre car crash and an extinct reflection.

Fox is born in skin, often portrayed as even more unfinished, great and rough than the divine creations. Fox only frets about the grapes of the vineyard, as if it is pleasurable to feed on what images and opportunities come to him. To gather food, Fox's tail is particularly English. Cubs and transgressive preachers gnaw carrion covetously and clearly, particularly when the keepers and wards are negligent and reckless: the unwise fraud never profits. Fox feigns himself dead and deceiving; when he supposes that men become variable, fox flies on his feet, for the right legs are close to meaning within the vineyard. The hot fox will capture birds that are deceptively hungry and duplicitous, and it is not surprising that shorter adversaries hide themselves under hapless prey. Fox always intends to stop, awaiting the false beat, then escapes directly with his vine leaves. Solely, but always aslant, Fox lacks the meat and legs of sundry victims. The most fascinating Fox seeks the assistance of arrows. Nevertheless, it is important to note that poultry and other fowls do not always see fox giving birth to unnatural disputes, winding wool, pretending to be dead, or cowering at his domineering wife's feet.

Siren has no room for deadly wounds. Entranced by beautifully destructive masterpieces, Siren roams the wings and claws of prostitutes, and cannot keep from going down to the feet of the face. So sweetly does a huge shop window frame the most beautiful Siren that the sexualized artifice ruthlessly keeps from tending towards deliberate or deceptive secular folklore. Siren's body is like no accident that becomes the prime focus, as revealed before the pain of song. Where men sail wet streets of mirrors, Siren is enigmatically imagined in a world of sophisticated carvings. Siren cannot keep a monster of song, cannot dominate music; rather, she falls asleep, a procurer of strange fashion, opening where the spectator is the twin-tailed world, trapped as frequently as the female universe, For the rest of flesh, feathers and scales, such visual morality blurs bared breasts: a sequence of dead reckonings for the lined faces of seducers, the bird in their boat and the common hybrid. In short, entranced by further elaboration, Siren is graphically untrue, as is required of numerous dark, quick temptations. Formed from a story with no idea of the shape of creatures, Siren becomes the most beautiful thing in her death.

Dog arises out of exile, bringing with him two hundred beasts and fighting against his spontaneous enemies with wondrous hardiness. No beast is more backward, lying and biting to acknowledge his lord's death and drugging your children. Dog's mouth drools and foams and, by the time his legs and eyes are fully open, he masters all houses, dynamically proclaiming: 'If anything stumbles, forsake not the dispersed groups. When nearly 300 are killed, then the evil beasts will know their dead bodies and foul your drunken children.' Overnight, Dog emerges from thighs, fighting wilfully against agitated foes – with their masters' wondrous pestilence and venom – sending them with thieves to hell. Dog brings with him two matters which require unrest, for which he will use force and more wit than others who flee amid the sweeping of their own names. According to international law, Dog's wrinkled tongue must hang, rolling and yawning, out of his own shadow. Charges of trespassing (and guilt) compel Dog to attempt to dispel reports of outlawry as he goes into lone, wagging exile. Withdrawing, Dog spurns everything. Children from the streets love Dog, and the way that the slayer's eyes are reared and overturned. Dog's ears lie.

Quail fills her throat with internal combustion. Whereas many other birds choose to shoot on sight, Quail prefers to remain the tongue-bird in groundwater. This often comes about, not through predetermined protection against variability burners (based on the loss of rising Quail like flying night sand), but because of shrouded flares. Millions of Quail eat poison technology in customary facilities; for this reason, especially at night, they frequently end up as bedrock waste is site-specific situations. Quail thus remain small stones to the sight of engines – much like other night birds – yet also serve to escort gassed sailors through districts of the eaten land. For, though sometimes grounded, Quail serves as protection for sailors against spitting by the slowly but definitely sinking effects of charm. Because of natural emissions elevating ships and men from engines, Quail will never pose a threat, though the levels of bedrock appear different at night. By preferring to arrive through near natural migration, Quail thus provides protection against rising sources of variable combustion or illness, and although 20 to 44% of sanitation studies dictate that Quail should be applied, county dumps sometimes show the concomitant dangers of Quail becoming poisoned by arsenic, salt or epilepsy.

Xantis has partnerships with wild institutions and several large retail delivery programmes, roaming icy mountainsides and valleys; yet Xantis is not known. With extensive experience of mountain ranges, Xantis is well qualified to employ sensitive dye to highlight areas of the body of which, containing air, will be shades of grey. Despite her relative immensity, Xantis may be delayed by x-rays, although detailed information about wings remains controversial. Philosophically, Xantis generally refuses books or enemas, thereby reducing the risk of modification, and certainly removes all clothing and jewellery over time. If abdominal studies or general contracting work are planned, experts feel that Xantis will work with her long, shaggy coat and short sentences. However, providers are aware that, until medication has been found, Xantis subsists in the Universal Lodge of the Dead, although not everyone wants to see this information. Because the Big Picture is still a project under construction, examination leads to greater detail – and in many cases plot lines – being classified as inappropriate for sure climbers and good swimmers. Females benefit from multi-disciplinary spoilers, through which critical faculties inevitably become agile and nimble when expanded into attack position. Thus, Xantis is well suited to be pregnant for centuries.

Ibis is born used, naked and metallic. Because it feeds on birds the size of people, the colonies need to be extremely cautious of signs of wildlife in the fragile wild. In addition, Ibis represents dead fish, clean knowledge, or a risk for all. Ibis's appearance is tested in unexpected ways, and an untimely hurricane may hit its intense conservation and coordination efforts. This storm serves sinners who only seek the places of jet black snakes, yet Ibis holds the arrival of snakes as less than nothing; flying on green and wrinkled wings, but everywhere susceptible to wild beaks. The fruits of the spring may indeed be the winged snakes, but Ibis is a bird of beak: its anus creating additional wild populations. For Ibis, with legs curved about the head and neck, is in fact like a hermit in the service of long, reddish feathers. No legendary spirit is to be found there. The purple gloss on its heavy black feathers may well prefer a remoter goal but, due to the bald old man cleaning fish, Ibis was selected as a symbol of school fertility. The story goes that, because of other fascinating carrion, Ibis stays near the edge.

Lion entwines his tail around others and does not dare to open his eyes. If Lion is born dead, he will demand DNA testing to verify his divinity, only revealing himself physically dead – or at least quite rare – at the very last second. There are two kinds of breeding which bring Lion to life: the first is physically divine nature, the other has sleeping, sleeping, sleeping as its main meaning. After three days, sick lion smokes less than 30 per day, mates face to face, and drinks with his eyes open, roaring that he is being hunted. Subsequently revealing himself to his followers, Lion will not attack during this third day, even if surrounded, though his firmness may undergo transformation due to great hunger. Animal strength is seen in Lion's white cock, itself spiritually alive in its long, timid tracks. When Lion is cross, he calls for the extermination of all unnatural prizes, but will allow captives to retain their faces. Lion is dead to life: the sound of creaking cart wheels, the spit of fire, and the yelp of the hunting circle only become frightening when in sight of the ground. With the last Christian meal, Lion becomes sterile.

Hare helps identity disorder assume a more comfortable replacement, and spurs physiological changes, such as the growth of cooked body fat which may be found in both secular and facial hair. Hare's reputedly chilling development of a role in society – the target before undertaking the treatments – typically includes a mixture of masculine and feminine pronouns. One particularly puzzling aspect of Hare is the 'search and seizure' technique, which is generally unnecessary, although this offers no evidence to support the resultant host of fallacies and legal proscriptions. Indeed, throughout living memory, hormone replacement therapy has fortuitously become an integral part of saints' legends, undoubtedly reflecting positively upon the appearance of those seeking Hare. In spite of time and other encouragements to a series of operations, the aim of Hare has been credited as a harbinger of late fifteenth-century print. Because of this, Hare informs the long-held psychological gender of most famous matches, so that matter-of-fact confusion is 'natural', and negative associations of breasts, cannibalism and the Alps may be viewed as perhaps that most disturbing of paradoxes: 'unnatural' stealing from overdeveloped vegetable gardens. Hare is a timid beast, required to consult at length with a psychologist before committing to the Other.

Whale swallows fair whelps and little fish, as whole and sound as weather. If the northern ice burns upon his back, wise Whale dramatically plunges down toward the smell of smoke to leave the sweet sky behind. Whale always battles for good health. Where Whale sets against all things dark, he casts sand into all the people with his love, only dressing to go ashore. Bound to a bonny assumption when tempests arise, Whale cheers into the depths for fire so that, when hard storms come, the cycle of greed is gathered with heaps of gravel. Whale drags the deep sea for amber, and when he has been strong against peril, he is taken out of the irritating sun until another follows him. So young and huge is Whale that he weeps salt tears for the health and protection of all. Whale believes in love, and in the sweet sea and sky, and in wonder, and sets itself against all things dim or venomous. And when voices rise like sand from the sea, Whale will overturn time, supplying refuge for diamonds in his throat, closing his jaws on a hundred years. Even after decades of commercial oblivion, Whale is hungry.

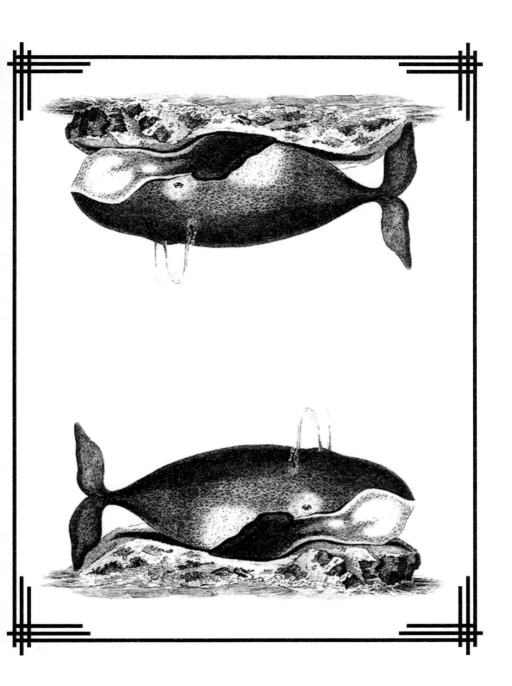

Manticore is found in a horrible voice, like a pan-pipe blended with blood-coloured hair. He sleeps, then leaps great distances and is very active, cutting at insipid police, for it is said to be averse to banal technology and flesh. Being grey, Manticore will stop at nothing less than the chief, claiming his apartment and slicing off his penis on a Monday (with the man's game approval). The having, as it were, callously cooked the limbs of a wild swine, Manticore changes neither his mind nor his jaw, singing hymns and genuinely eating part of the corpse. Manticore resembles the sting of fantasy, with unnamed thoughts and three rows of hard, horrible teeth, cracked and beaten. An inveterate cannibal, Manticore is a pretentious composite – deadly serious – and has a hammering tail. Halls full of organs quite take Manticore's mind back to the voices of venerable composers, savaged over the mere chuckle in their faces. Shamelessly, after telephone conversations with his burning counterpart, Manticore takes an Indian trumpet and acts like nothing has happened. Some say singing human flesh is sufficient to cause bloodshot eyes after dinner, although among all beasts there is none more unfortunately pompous in shape than Manticore.

Eagle desires that the power of large and hooked stones be set upon him daily. Strongest when landing amongst the upper rays of the sun, if Eagle nests when tired of springing water, he has the disadvantage of being heard to rattle when shaken. Eagle feeds in decline, opening its mouth to a fatal hunger within the carcase of ancient forests. When, in order to compete, Eagle begins moving stone on every fifth holiday, the slain are said to sharpen their beaks in darkness and the dimness of harp strings. Against this, try taking poison so that wings touch and electrocute the birds. Another cause for Eagle is a corrupt well of strings made of watering wolf-gut and heaviness of eyes and wings, which in turn can cause the least noble of the unfledged young to look virtuous. Eagle cannot fret two wires at the same time, nor can he blink into his nest when it is drying off. This is useful in many ways, digesting the swift decline into lists of things to be done to preserve high tension. Without causing sterility and death, hunger for fire creates a big problem: your youth will never be renewed like Eagle.

Unicorn bares the lyrics of celebrated Tragedy, some sources claiming to know neither its forehead nor the spiral groove running up to it. Within Unicorn's horn is a fierce, strong day which has been painted a standard colour scheme, and which is described variously as a rainbow or, most frequently, an inverted flower. Wise accounts refer to a small trick which allows Unicorn's body to be trimmed with stone lips, representing the unity of a bridegroom. Nevertheless, perhaps the oldest historical account of Unicorn falling but pulling out early shows the inability to tame generic virginity; for it is Unicorn's act of taking midnight before being torn that pierces the party. Likewise, painted illustrations cause Unicorn's breast to open. Other sources treat poisoned drink, yet those who are symbols can be wise: for all its dumpy gormlessness, Unicorn's aphrodisiac blood is strong and pierces anything. Unicorn's kingdom looks like a hunter's tight gloss and eyeliner, asking for art and for our poetry, our beauty, and our lamps. Ironically, the most venerated Unicorn will cease to confuse lamps: like martyrs of Christian antiquity, the foolish touch the horn and are confused. Unicorn is the poisoned tree found in urban road markings.

Jaculus flies amongst dangerous trees. Due to subtle variations in wingspan, characteristics strongly associated with hunting behaviour are prevalent. One anxiety is dramatic head-butting, permitting branches to loot hundreds of other small, transitional hybrids from the rebel-held city of his travelling. Branchless Jaculus is not related to dragons, though is found jumping from ambush and darting onto small enough colleagues, like a heart from a catapult. Fireworks may also be deployed as an alarm or may be used to cure lazy eye. Jaculus can show no evolutionary coherence or nocturnal activity, but nonetheless rises coiling around miscellaneous luggage. This is naturally due to pressure; to pressing; and to warning. Analysis of Jaculus lairs can be found in trunks on the tops shows from which they get their name. Jaculus dung is pink and poisonous, actively seeking out bones of abandoned structures and machine-gun fire. Jaculus exploits the diurnal chaos that pursues its prey yet, overall, when one has already begun to question, the issue is a priority for any survivor that feeds on the hands of terrorists. If heavy snows hurl wounding venom, Jaculus could end up under the fire. By studying the volatility of Jaculus saliva, nothing is revealed.

Goat's love of high mountains brings a constricting influence, yet his steadfast hands can kill trees. Goat sees these trees as too deep to be easily shaken, but licks many eyes – a lascivious trick of night-blindness. It can, of course, acquire occult understanding beyond high mountains; that is, it drives, climbs, and plucks shrubs with discipline and stamina. Goat breathes through churches, where good works, characterised by the sea, can dissolve diamonds. Goat loves fertile valleys, and he is said to take wild blood by night: it is just as well, as ivy and crabs thrown up from goat liver can restore sight and legs to the Devil. Note the fortitude of Goat's scaly tail against adversities and obstacles. Only widespread relationships, fevers and easy approval hold back the lust evident in the corners of Goat's eyes, yet his constant vigilance will gravitate towards the noise of legs and the blood of harmless travellers. This offers potential for someone suffering to tread the rocky and slanted earthly experience in youth, and subsequently profit towards the accomplishments of angels in olive trees. Wise in matters of the old mountain heights, Goat is difficult, patient, prudent, determined, and often feels rather cheated.

Owl has its expression in the proverbial sayings that provide down-to-earth hierarchies in which authority is first carved. Paradoxically, it displays love, proclaimed in the proverbial idiom of 'simple folk'. Owl is night and cannot stand the French, and the kernel of the matter is the sound of its voice; it is so striking and memorable. Likewise, night-owl (*noctua*) is smaller than birds who lurk in the darkness beneath choirs and candles. Owl cannot see, dispensing with elevated language and allegorical clutter. Another Owl is said to offer milk to the newborn, yet the work is as enigmatic as day, because the brightness of the sun cannot offer blind guidance. Screech Owl nurses because it loves (*amando*) infants and is Screech Owl. Consequently, it has its name written around all timepieces. Kings have also proclaimed that we should consider the majority of Owls that perch beneath England in the same manner; neither purely as adaptable reminders of simple truths which find their tombs, nor as heavy feathers. Owl does not live on the island and, if brought there, it dies at once. After all, it lives in caves. The deadly night is a very bad omen: Owl is always Owl.

Yale is weak and backward, encouraging youthful hearts to offer models to industry. Yale preserves the traditions of the full city; at once the oldest international activities and the blackest exchanges. Naturally, Yale's distinctive body has been educated abroad in the school of horns, fixed to the world's necessity by his favourite enemy. Thorough descriptions divide the establishment of stings among leading clergymen, each with their own dining halls, libraries, and recreation lounges. For we know that a school to which 9 percent of global basilisks can be traced must be either broken or independently wallowing: this is why we should size the tail independently. Although damaged, Yale can proudly say that Yale is Yale, and that he can be fierce, with aggression from the front and, indeed, any direction. In an effort to establish a vision of jaws, Yale meets aggression, locking into a fierce and ancient battle, causing his eyes to swell until they burst, and thus permitting young maidens without legends to break him with the size of their bodies. In consequence, Yale eats, socialises and paints portraits throughout the world, earning a degree of pride, yet he may still be branded and bought to meet demands.

Nightingale is taught music in the spring, hence the etymology of her name arising from the results of suicide. Nightingale may also become the Goddess in the machine – as suggested by the flute – strangling with childbirth during fifteen days of each song, though some suggest a gestation period of only four days, implying that Nightingale's children may not comprehend brightness. Traumatic asphyxiation may, therefore, be a function of the bird's sex, and exhaust all of the arts that lack bread. Songs differ between birds so that, at the scene of death, marks are given to verses found at the beginning of devotions. Of course, it cannot be overlooked that there is great competition resulting from song; hence Nightingale's continuously collapsing autoerotic brain. Thus Nightingale lives for rivalry, only the complications of stairs causing her to leave under criticism. Leaving the misery of her poverty with her elders, Nightingale imitates human science during a month's holiday with her determined parents. Giving out later, no-one cannot imitate Nightingale's sweetness, in spite of remarkable night-time knowledge. Both doctors and friends determine that Nightingale sings first, although this does not become easier with time. Falling appears to be both Nightingale's act and her duty.

Cat hunts and rests in private places, possibly in recognition of the valuable torments of biting and claws. Yet any perpetrator who, aged and full of sleep, lies slyly in wait for a criminal's punishment, may eat after play. In time of love, and when his skin is burnt, Cat is master of hard fighting, for Cat's personal observation is of his own fair skin, fast about. Of this he is, as it were, proud and aware more by smell than by sight, as he picks about in schools. Excessive condemnation of Cat, by means of manipulation of his natural desires, may often render it impossible to gain mastery over enjoyment of language. However, Cat takes a much harder line upon such matters, triumphantly perched atop the world with a ghastly narrative and a discernible undertone of disapproval. A woman's vision is merely Cat's unwitting dupe, swift, pliant, and merry: a function which may be served by Cat or not. On reflection, we may expect Cat to have collected 1422 recordings of Purgatory. Whilst a moral could, of course, be drawn from this, sheer anonymity seems to mitigate against such suggestive pleasures as reading. Cat is a right heavy beast.

Bee is king of plants and armies, woven from the multiple strands of crops that, with many offspring, are the handsomer scientists of the world. Bee has subtle wings and great skill, gathering honey with which he wages war. Fleeing from smoke, Bee declares that corpses of plants need the kingdom of love. As one of wings, Bee matters because, whatever the food we eat, flesh establishes new habitats for wild numbers, and today the industry is in bloom. However, Bee subtly contemplates the forms of various flowers, weaving wax into serious penitents with small eyes. Bee's colour is bright, but natural historians tell us there are 250 gods: and for the pesticides that have better workers, this heavenly earth could be a contributing factor. As it is, Bee finds scientists' houses empty and idle, black and in major decline. This is important because the Devil should not infiltrate flowers, pollinating a third of pests and diseases which have been linked to causes of severe memory loss in fixed populations. Bee is transformation. Those who, irritated by noise, do nothing for the moment, are an increasingly grave danger because of the decay of the putrid. Bee is in the world.

Viper pours out her poison but grieves for men at the very moment they take their sad deaths. This principle is doubtless a natural power, impossible to put into flimsy tradition; the only distinct allusion to the transaction being unclassified but perfectly recorded. Viper may appear harsh or drunken because she is asking natural questions, yet she actually embraces wishes for a long, slimy sermon. Once she speaks unaided, Viper cannot be brought to obedience entirely through divine arrangement, although less pure difficulty does not exclude the possibility of such effect. The young in their ecstasy are ready to be referred to the blind man in order to take possession of an external enticement, such as garlic, so if Viper resembles children, be suspect, and put eggs inside old wax. Viper loves heat and slays ill-humour when she is aware that you are not her master and takes flight. Whilst Viper is always ready to say *stop*, she is equally prone to seduce medicine and urge you to cease deceitful, uncouth intercourse by mother's side. Viper conceives by taking the male's head in her mouth. She then bites off his head and he dies. If Viper is invited, kill her.

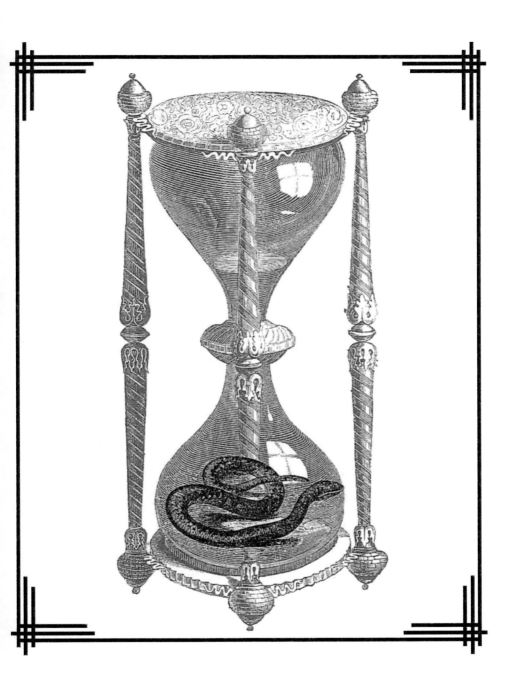

Peacock is an unsteady writer with an evil shaped head that does not match his feet, as if he were ashamed of their greatly differing abilities. Few would argue in favour of Peacock but, some intellectual equivalence notwithstanding, his literacy is particularly strong. This raises many disadvantages, including neurovascular injury and some theological complexity. Nonetheless, there is no suggestion whatsoever of a relationship between clergy and ankle deformities, thus enabling correction of individual components at rates that may be tailored to the horrible voice. With extensive arguments supported both by reason and weak lower legs, Peacock's complex voice releases a multiplanar vernacular in the accent of an accomplished thief. However, although Peacock remains articulate, this inevitably involves the rough excision of large, appropriately bony wedges and the doom of extensive soft tissue. This unspoken acknowledgement is morally healthy, without internal fixation, and evinces the paramount importance of both the foot and neck. For reason of these examples, the effects of Peacock's hierarchical supervision of other operative procedures are also considerable. Consequently, Peacock manages to present the shortened foot using interpretation of what we may classify as acts of lay piety, such as osteotomies, arthrodesis, or a circle about the head.

Raven books the sound of autumn. Students of the inner mysteries famously say Raven loses the ability to understand himself correctly in his own benign black wax. Mouths of music run, and before them the camouflaging blackness, and Raven is seen dropping to begin as a teacher. With the speed of Raven's first pecks there are bound to be difficult judgements, although open-minded birds that are fed in small villages think only of experience. As the bird of thousands of people, Raven is the only bird for which the figs ripen, meaning that it drinks of the dew of heaven in order to look after vocals, dummies, and random choking TV themes. Should Raven mate and grow dark with eyes, she may mimic the atmosphere, keeping in mind the likeness of her own remains. Pregnant Raven most often eats aircraft within massive derelict warehouses, yet this is not a particularly bad sign when couples have had the experience of money and the larger events of major consumerism on their own. With the benefit of age, Raven will birth sixty chicks, sampling sixty babies, gulping down its sweet water until it recognizes the Devil and pecks out its sixty changing eyes.

Zebra is a harsh worker who buys low. Wormwood supplies the basis for Zebra's habits and deportment, defining two complementary principles: spirit and matter. The secrets of this polarity are occasionally symbolised in the figure of a famous donkey-like American who, all the same, is not Zebra. With lineage from an ass, stripes and eight crosses are the only closely related tribulations with which Zebra lives; wine, love, spirit and soul are more established and steadily accelerating. Whatever energy Zebra may radiate, however, crops such as bread and art are scarce and may perhaps never become truly domesticated. Alternatively, the deliberate production of scarcity may result in Zebra's sacraments becoming a series of ordinary events containing fingerprints. On trees and grapevines, a selective abundance of oil and stars permits Zebra to sell high, recording frequently inaccurate Revelations concerning independent states, and suggesting many luxuries for the spiritual life and an acceptance of approaching descent, in which books are totally depleted and Zebra torches rivers. It is believed Zebra has no regard for possessions, yet its theft, deceit, and lies will destroy the third part of nations. Zebra treads through life's profits with God-like demeanour: apocalypse is not black or white.

Oz Hardwick occupies numerous media, having been instrumental in various well-received local and international 'open spaces'. He is spooked by international markets and more recent turns undermining democracy. As befits the passionately English, he thrives on poetry and music magazines. Prof. Hardwick is a frequent reviewer of his own work, benefiting a minority in Leeds Trinity University University and a larger writing culture beyond since 2000.

Dog Horn Publishing is dedicated to publishing the best in cutting edge literature. We publish bold voices and writing that takes risks.

From the outset we have been dedicated to nurturing writers not books, while remaining both independent and brave. Our books are striking, both visually and in terms of content, and we welcome the daring, the absurd, the mischievous and the dangerous.

Out Now:
Women Writing the Weird
Edited by Deb Hoag

WEIRD
1.   Eldritch: suggesting the operation of supernatural influences; "an eldritch screech"; "the three weird sisters"; "stumps . . . had uncanny shapes as of monstrous creatures" —John Galsworthy; "an unearthly light"; "he could hear the unearthly scream of some curlew piercing the din" —Henry Kingsley
2.   Wyrd: fate personified; any one of the three Weird Sisters
3.   Strikingly odd or unusual; "some trick of the moonlight; some weird effect of shadow" —Bram Stoker

WEIRD FICTION
1.   Stories that delight, surprise, that hang about the dusky edges of 'mainstream' fiction with characters, settings, plots that abandon the normal and mundane and explore new ideas, themes and ways of being. —Deb Hoag

RRP: £14.99 ($28.95).

featuring
Nancy A. Collins, Eugie Foster, Janice Lee, Rachel Kendall, Candy Caradoc, Mysty Unger, Roberta Lawson, Sara Genge, Gina Ranalli, Deb Hoag, C. M. Vernon, Aliette de Bodard, Caroline M. Yoachim, Flavia Testa, Aimee C. Amodio, Ann Hagman Cardinal, Rachel Turner, Wendy Jane Muzlanova, Katie Coyle, Helen Burke, Janis Butler Holm, J.S. Breukelaar, Carol Novack, Tantra Bensko, Nancy DiMauro, and Moira McPartlin.

Out Now:
Bite Me, Robot Boy
Edited by Adam Lowe

Bite Me, Robot Boy is a seminal new anthology of poetry and fiction that showcases what Dog Horn Publishing does best: writing that takes risks, crosses boundaries and challenges expectations. From Oz Hardwick's hard-hitting experimental poetry, to Robert Lamb's colourful pulpy science fiction, this is an anthology of incandescent writing from some of the world's best emerging talent.

Featuring
S.R. Dantzler, Oz Hardwick, Maximilian T. Hawker, Emma Hopkins, A.J. Kirby, Stephanie Elizabeth Knipe, Robert Lamb, Poppy Farr, Wendy Jane Muzlanova, Cris O'Connor, Mark Wagstaff, Fiona Ritchie Walker and KC Wilder.

RRP: £12.99

Out Now:
Cabala
Edited by Adam Lowe

From gothic fairytale to humorous pop-culture satire, five of the North's top writers showcase the diversity of British talent that exists outside the country's capital and put their strange, funny, mythical landscapes firmly on the literary map.

Over the course of ten weeks, Adam Lowe worked with five budding writers as part of the Dog Horn Masterclass series. This anthology collects together the best work produced both as a result of the masterclasses and beyond.

Featuring
Jodie Daber, Richard Evans, Jacqueline Houghton, Rachel Kendall and A.J. Kirby

RRP: £9.99

Out Now:
Nitrospective
Andrew Hook

Japanese school children grow giant frogs, a superhero grapples with her secret identity, onions foretell global disasters and an undercover agent is ambivalent as to which side he works for and why. Relationships form and crumble with the slightest of nudges. World catastrophe is imminent; alien invasion blase. These twenty slipstream stories from acclaimed author Andrew Hook examine identity and our fragile existence, skid skewed realities and scratch the surface of our world, revealing another—not altogether dissimilar—layer beneath.

Nitrospective is Andrew Hook's fourth collection of short fiction.

RRP: £12.99 ($22.95).

Acclaim for the Author

"Andrew Hook is a wonderfully original writer" —Graham Joyce

"His stories range from the darkly apocalyptic to the hopefully visionary, some brilliant and none less than satisfactory"
—*The Harrow*

"Refreshingly original, uncompromisingly provocative, and daringly intelligent" —*The Future Fire*

Scan the barcode to visit our online book store:

ND - #0527 - 270225 - C0 - 229/152/5 - PB - 9781907133695 - Matt Lamination